Wait! *WHAT?*

LUCILLE BALL Had No Eyebrows?

DAN GUTMAN

illustrated by **ALLISON STEINFELD**

NORTON YOUNG READERS

An Imprint of W. W. Norton & Company
Celebrating a Century of Independent Publishing

To kids who like to learn cool stuff.

Copyright © 2023 by Dan Gutman
Illustrations copyright © 2023 by Allison Steinfeld

All rights reserved
Printed in the United States of America
First Edition

For information about permission to reproduce selections from this book, write to
Permissions, W. W. Norton & Company, Inc., 500 Fifth Avenue, New York, NY 10110

For information about special discounts for bulk purchases, please contact W. W. Norton
Special Sales at specialsales@wwnorton.com or 800-233-4830

Manufacturing by Lake Book Manufacturing
Book design by Hana Anouk Nakamura
Production manager: Delaney Adams

ISBN 978-1-324-03072-0 (cl)
978-1-324-03073-7 (pbk)

W. W. Norton & Company, Inc.
500 Fifth Avenue, New York, N.Y. 10110
www.wwnorton.com

W. W. Norton & Company Ltd.
15 Carlisle Street, London W1D 3BS

1 2 3 4 5 6 7 8 9 0

CONTENTS

That's True, But . . .

I'll tell you what's *really* interesting—celebrities. Everybody likes to read about famous people.

The problem is that all the biographies for kids always leave out the *good* stuff. The cool stuff.

Yeah, so we decided to learn about famous people and write about them. But we leave out all the boring junk and just include the good parts. This time, we're taking on the actress Lucille Ball. Let's just call her Lucy to make it easy.

Y'know, I never even *heard* of that lady until we started working on this book.

Wait! WHAT? She was probably the most famous woman in the world. Just about everybody watched her TV show *I Love Lucy*. Newsweek called her "probably the most popular woman in the history of show business." The U.S. Postal Service put her picture on a stamp. She was named one of the ten most admired women in the world, ahead of Queen Elizabeth! She has *two* stars on the Hollywood Walk of Fame! She received the

Presidential Medal of Freedom! *TV Guide* voted her the Greatest TV Star of All Time! And you never heard of her?

Okay, I get it. Chill. I know lots about her now, and I watched a bunch of episodes of *I Love Lucy*. But you left out the most important Lucy fact of all.

What's that?

She had no eyebrows.

Yeah, I couldn't help but notice the title of the book. Would you like to explain?

No.

Come on! You can't just throw out something like that without explaining it. Was she born without eyebrows? Did they get burned off in a fire or something?

No, it was neither of those things. Okay, okay, I'll tell you what happened. Before she was ever on TV, Lucy acted in lots of movies. Back in those days, the movie studios would control the way actresses looked. They'd dye their hair, make them lose weight, make them wear certain clothes or wigs, and stuff like that. And one thing they did was shave off their eyebrows.

Why? That's the dumbest thing I ever heard of.

Think about it. What purpose do eyebrows serve anyway? Why do we even *have* eyebrows in the first place?

I don't know! Hey, can we argue about that another time? Why did they shave off Lucille Ball's eyebrows?

In the 1940s it was the fashion for women to have really skinny eyebrows. People thought it was a good look. So they'd shave off the actress's eyebrows and then draw in fake eyebrows with an eyebrow pencil.

Okay, that's just weird. But don't eyebrows just grow back after they get shaved off?

Not always! Lucille Ball's eyebrows never grew back. So she had to draw in her own eyebrows for the rest of her life.

Wow. Now, that *is* an amazing fact. How did you find that out?

I did my research, just like you!

Well, I did *tons* of research on Lucille Ball. I dug up all kinds of cool facts like that, and you won't see them in other books for kids.

You want to hear another strange fact about Lucille Ball?

I'm listening.

She received radio signals through her teeth.

Very funny. Now you're just being silly. Let's move on to the next chapter.

Fine. Be that way. But it's true!

You're crazy. Okay, how did she receive radio signals through her teeth? *This* I want to hear.

You hurt my feelings. So I'm not going to tell you.

You're impossible!

"In life, all good things come hard, but wisdom is the hardest to come by."

CHAPTER I

Stuff Your Teacher Wants You to Know About Lucille Ball . . .

August 6, 1911 Lucille Désirée Ball is born in Jamestown, New York.

March 2, 1917 Desi Arnaz is born in Santiago de Cuba.

1926 Lucy, fifteen years old, travels to New York City to attend the John Murray Anderson School for the Dramatic Arts. After a month, she goes back home.

1928 Lucy returns to New York and works as a model for dress designer Hattie Carnegie. She comes down with rheumatic fever and goes back home.

1932 Lucy comes to New York *again*, to become an actress and model.

1933 Lucy goes to Hollywood and appears in her first movie. Desi Arnaz escapes Cuba and comes to the United States.

1940 Lucy appears in the movie *Too Many Girls*, meets Desi Arnaz, and marries him.

1948 Lucy stars in the radio sitcom *My Favorite Husband*.

July 17, 1951 Daughter Lucie Arnaz is born.

October 15, 1951 *I Love Lucy* is broadcast on CBS Television. It becomes the number-one show on TV.

January 19, 1953 Son Desi Arnaz Jr. is born.

1957 *I Love Lucy* ends.

1960 Lucy and Desi get divorced.

1961 Lucy marries Gary Morton.

1962 Lucy becomes the first woman to run a major TV studio. *The Lucy Show* begins, and runs until 1968.

1968 *Here's Lucy* begins, and runs until 1974.

1985 Lucy appears in her final movie, *Stone Pillow*.

1986 *Life With Lucy* begins, and ends. Desi Arnaz dies on December 2.

April 26, 1989 Lucy dies.

2001 Lucy is inducted into the National Women's Hall of Fame. The U.S. Postal Service issues a stamp to celebrate what would have been her ninetieth birthday.

2008 *TV Guide* ranks *I Love Lucy* the second-best TV show ever.

2021 Nicole Kidman and Javier Bardem, as Lucy and Desi, are nominated for Oscars for the movie *Being the Ricardos*.

Are you still awake? Fantastic! Okay, let's get to the *good* stuff, the stuff your *teacher* doesn't even know about Lucille Ball.

I thought teachers know *everything* about everything.

They know *almost* everything. But not *this* stuff!

Okay, let's get to it.

"Life takes guts."

This Book Is a Bummer

We should probably start at the beginning.

Do we have to? That beginning stuff is always boring.

It doesn't *have* to be boring! Listen to this: Lucille Ball was descended from some of the earliest settlers of the thirteen colonies, and she was very possibly related to George Washington.

Get out!

No, really. George Washington's mother's maiden name was Mary Ball.

You don't say!

I say. Not only that, but Lucille Ball was a descendant of one of the women accused of being a witch during the Salem witch trials in 1692.

I didn't know that.

Okay, are you in the mood to be depressed?

No.

Well, too bad. Because Lucille Ball's childhood is *really* depressing. Her mother's name was Désirée, but everybody called her DeDe. Her father's name was Henry, but everybody called him Had. He worked for the telephone company, and the family had to move around a lot for his job.

What's so depressing about that?

Well, Lucy's father died when she was just three years old.

Oh.

He got typhoid fever, and he was just twenty-eight years old. Lucy's mother was a widow when she was twenty-two.

That must have been horrible.

Lucy and Birds

Yeah, and that day was Lucy's first memory. She remembered that on the day her father died, a bird flew into an open window of her house and got trapped in there. From that moment on, and for the rest of her life, Lucy was afraid of birds.

I read about that. She would never stay in a hotel that had pictures of birds on the wall. One time, she bought some expensive silk wallpaper for her home. It wasn't until it was up on the wall that she noticed there were birds in the design. The wallpaper was taken down the next day.

And you know what's really odd? One of the most famous bird artists—Roger Tory Peterson—grew up in the same town as Lucy: Jamestown, New York. Anyway, when Had died, DeDe was pregnant with Lucy's little brother, Fred, and she had her hands full. To make sure Lucy didn't run around the neighborhood, DeDe tied a dog leash around her waist—

Wait! WHAT?

—and she attached the other end of the leash to a clothesline in the backyard. When Lucy ran around playing, she would pull on the leash and it made a noise. So if there was no noise, DeDe would run outside to make sure Lucy was okay.

That doesn't sound like much fun.

Oh, it gets worse. DeDe suffered from terrible headaches. She would lie in a dark room with the shades down. She couldn't move or talk. It got so bad that Lucy's grandparents sent DeDe to live in California and they took care of Lucy and her brother.

DeDe fell in love with a man named Ed Peterson out there, and when they got married a few years later, Lucy and her brother were sent to live with *his* parents.

Why *them*?

Beats me. But they were really strict, serious people. They only had one mirror in the whole house, because they thought mirrors were a sign

of being vain. One time they caught Lucy
looking at herself in the mirror, and she was
sent to her room.

I bet that's why she invented Sassafrassa and
Madeline the Cowgirl.

What? Who were they?

Lucy's imaginary friends. They were dolls she

made out of clothespins, and she would talk to them. She had a fantasy world in her imagination, and that helped her deal with the situation she was in. She lived with Grandma Peterson from age eight to twelve.

Eventually, Lucy's mom came back home to raise her. But it was a tough way to grow up. Before Lucy was ten years old, her father died, her mother was gone for over three years, and she lived in eight different places.

Plus, she grew up *really* poor. Her house had no hot water. They would heat water on a wood-burning stove. During the summer, she and her brother would take a bar of soap to a nearby lake so they could wash themselves. When she was older, Lucy remembered the "glorious day" her first bathtub arrived.

The Ball family was so poor that Lucy couldn't afford a pencil to bring to school with her. For the rest of her life, she hoarded pencils wherever she went.

Wow, she was one of the funniest people in the world, but this book looks like it's going to be a total bummer.

Be patient. Even though times were really hard, Lucy found that she really loved getting attention. As a little kid, she would go to the local grocery store, hop up on the counter, and pretend to be a frog. The customers would give her pennies.

That was her first professional performance.

When Lucy was twelve, her stepfather suggested she try out for a local theater company. She got a part in a play, and she loved it. Even though she dislocated her shoulder when another actor threw her across the stage, she decided that she wanted a career in show business.

And then she became a movie star, right?

Uh, no. When she was fifteen, Lucy started going out with a boy who was much older than she was. Her mother disapproved. So do you know what DeDe did?

She told the boy to get lost and never come back?

No, she sent Lucy to acting school in New York City, which was six hundred miles away. So Lucy got on a bus and arrived in New York with fifty dollars sewn into her underwear.

🧑 Wait a minute. If somebody sews money into your underwear, how do you get it out?

👩 I don't know! I guess you have to rip the stitches or something. That's not important!

🧑 But if your money is sewn into your underwear and you want to buy an ice-cream cone or something for a few dollars, you have to take your pants off, rip out the stitches from your underwear, and get the money!

👩 I guess so. Who cares? Anyway, even though Lucy loved acting, she hated acting school. The school didn't like her either. After a month, they sent her mom a letter saying she was wasting her money by sending her daughter to acting school. They said Lucy had no talent.

🧑 Ouch. That must have hurt. So what did she do?

👩 She took the bus back home and went to high school. She was a cheerleader, she played on the

20

basketball team, and she
loved riding horses and
ice-skating.

During the summer, she
flipped hamburgers at the
snack bar of an amusement park. She
would shout at people walking by,
"Don't step there! Step over
here and get yourself a
delicious hamburger!"

While she was in high
school, Lucy kept on
performing. She and two
of her friends formed a
musical group called "The Gloom Chasers
Union." Lucy was the drummer.

Never heard of 'em.

Nobody did. After that, Lucy and her friends
formed their own acting company and put on
plays in the school gym at night. Lucy was the
writer, director, and lead actor. She also helped

make and sell tickets, print up posters, build props, and sweep up the stage at the end of the show.

The tickets cost twenty-five cents, and the girls made twenty-five dollars.

Did you read that when she was in high school, Lucy got so angry with one of her teachers that she threw a typewriter at her?

No. What's a typewriter?

You're kidding, right? You don't know what a typewriter is?

Uh. It's something you write on?

It was this machine they used to use before there were computers.

Oh yeah, I knew that.

Liar! Anyway, Lucy never finished high school.

Maybe she would have graduated if she hadn't thrown that typewriter at her teacher. But I bet things are going to get happier now, right?

No, something terrible happened. It was 1927. Lucy was sixteen. Her grandfather Fred was in the yard with a few of the neighborhood kids, showing them how to shoot a rifle.

Uh-oh. I think I know where this is heading.

He set up some cans for the kids to use for target practice. Grandpa Fred told the kids not to move while one of the kids got ready to shoot. Just as this girl was about to pull the trigger, the mother of one of the boys called out for her son to come home. He got up to leave and ran right in front of the target. The bullet hit him, and the boy was paralyzed.

Oh no!

Grandpa Fred was the only adult watching the kids. He got sued by the boy's family. He lost the lawsuit, lost his house, lost his life savings, and lost everything he owned. And when the boy died a few years later, Grandpa Fred had to live with the fact that he was responsible for the boy's death.

Oh man. Do we have to end the chapter like that?

Hey, life isn't all candy and laughter, Turner. Bad stuff happens.

Can we move on now? I can't take much more of this depressing stuff.

1825: Bolivia became an independent country.

1926: Nineteen-year-old Gertrude Ederle became the first woman to swim across the English Channel, breaking the men's record by almost two hours.

1945: The atomic bomb was dropped on Hiroshima, Japan.

1960: Chubby Checker sang "The Twist" on TV, starting a worldwide dance craze.

1962: Jamaica became an independent country.

1964: The world's oldest tree, 4,862 years old, was accidentally cut down in Nevada.

1965: President Lyndon Johnson signed the Voting Rights Act, prohibiting voting discrimination against minorities.

2012: NASA's robotic vehicle *Curiosity* landed on Mars and began sending back photos.

Other People Who Were Born on **LUCY'S BIRTHDAY**

+ Andy Warhol: Artist
+ Alexander Fleming: Scientist who discovered penicillin
+ Alfred, Lord Tennyson: British poet
+ Leslie Odom Jr.: Actor and singer
+ M. Night Shyamalan: Movie director
+ Dutch Schultz: Gangster
+ Edith Roosevelt: First Lady of the United States

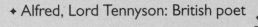

CHAPTER 3

Rats, Roaches, Jerks, and Horse Urine

Is this where the funny stuff starts?

Not by a long shot. After the shooting incident, Lucy decided to give New York City another try.

Oh yeah, this is when she became a model, right? I read about that. She was seventeen, and she wanted to get a fresh start, so she told everybody she was from Montana. She even wrote to the Montana Chamber of Commerce to get some facts about Montana so she would sound like she was telling the truth.

She changed her name too. She started calling herself Diane Belmont.

How did she come up with that?

She named herself after a horse-racing track called Belmont.

Aha. And she had no money, of course. She found a cheap apartment that was infested with rats and cockroaches.

Ugh.

When she climbed the stairs to her apartment, she would stamp her feet and sing to chase the critters away.

Lucy was so broke that she would make tomato soup from ketchup and hot water.

I read that one time she had to beg on the street for a penny because she only had four cents, and it cost a nickel to ride the subway. And to this day, people leave nickels on Lucy's gravestone.

She took any job she could find to make money. She sold cosmetics, she was an elevator operator in a department store—

Wait! WHAT? She was an elevator operator? What did she do, push the button?

I guess so. Back in the old days, you'd go into an elevator and tell the man or lady what floor you wanted to go to. Lucy also got a job as a soda jerk.

Soda jerk? What's that?

Back in the old days, people would go into a pharmacy and order a soda—

In a *pharmacy*?

Yeah. And the person behind the counter would pull on a handle to make the soda come out of a spigot. Then they might add a scoop of ice cream or syrup. They were called soda jerks.

Man, the old days were weird.

Anyway, Lucy was fired from that job when she served somebody a banana split but forgot to put in the banana.

Rookie mistake!

Eventually she got a job as a model. She modeled coats in a ladies' coat store. It paid thirty-five dollars a week.

That's when she dyed her hair, right?

Yeah. Lucy had naturally brown hair. But they thought she could sell more coats if she dyed her hair blonde, so she did. Anyway, things were moving along, and then another horrible thing happened.

Of *course*.

In the middle of a modeling session, Lucy suddenly felt terrible pain in her legs. She collapsed.

What happened?

Nobody knows exactly. Some books I read say it was rheumatoid arthritis. Others say it was rheumatic fever. Whatever it was, Lucy was taken to a medical clinic for the poor, because she only had eighty-five dollars to her name.

Oh yeah, and I know what was in the medicine they gave her.

What?

Horse urine!

No! For real?

Yeah, and the most amazing part is, the stuff worked! Lucy started feeling better, and she went home to Jamestown to recover. But it took two years until she was able to walk again. And after the whole thing was over, one of her legs was shorter than the other. She had to wear a twenty-pound weight in one of her shoes to fix the problem.

Okay, so after she recovered, she came back to New York City *again*. She started getting work as a model and was earning a hundred dollars a week.

And that was a lot of money in those days. It was the early 1930s, and it was the Depression.

So Lucy took this one job posing for an illustrator. She was wearing a blue chiffon dress, and the artist painted two Russian wolfhounds next to her. Well, it turned out that the company that made Chesterfield cigarettes was starting an ad campaign and they were looking for a flashy picture. They bought the painting of Lucy, and the next thing she knew, her face was on billboards all over New York City!

So I guess cigarettes weren't bad for *her* health, huh?

Very funny. Anyway, one day she was looking at herself on a billboard on Broadway when an agent recognized her. The agent told Lucy about a movie that Columbia Pictures was making in Hollywood. They needed to hire a dozen young women, and one of them had backed out. Three days later, Lucy was on a train to California.

It's about time she caught a break!

CHAPTER 4

Queen of the Bs

 Is this where the funny stuff starts?

Not yet. So Lucy was twenty-two. It was 1933 and she's in Tinseltown.

Why did they call it Tinseltown? Do they have a lot of Christmas trees in Los Angeles?

How should I know? It doesn't matter.

I thought you knew this stuff. There must be a reason why they called it Tinseltown.

Do I have to do everything? Look it up! Can we stay on topic? Lucy couldn't afford to buy a car, and she couldn't afford to take taxis. So she bought a bicycle for ten dollars.

I know the movie she auditioned for. *Roman Scandals*. It was about a delivery boy who gets bonked on the head, and when he wakes up he thinks he's in ancient Rome.

Yeah, and the star was this really famous actor named Eddie Cantor. Back in those days, they had lots of pretty girls standing around in the background of the movies, usually wearing bathing suits. Isn't that horrible?

Yeah. They could have had them wearing *space suits*. That would have been cool.

Never mind. Lucy was auditioning to be a slave girl. So there's this long row of young women lined up for Eddie Cantor to look over, and

Lucy wants to do something to get noticed. Do you know what she did?

She ripped up little pieces of red crepe paper and stuck them all over her face so it would look like she had measles.

How did you know that?!

I did my research! Eddie Cantor cracked up, Lucy got noticed, and she got the part in the movie. In her first scene, she was chased to a rock and accidentally fell twenty feet off a cliff. Another actor caught her just before she would have landed on some hot lights.

I'm impressed! So anyway, Lucy starts getting small parts like that in movies. Her contract with Columbia Pictures was for seven years, so she called up her mother and convinced her to move to California. In fact, she convinced her to bring Lucy's brother, grandfather, and cousin too.

So the whole family could be together.

And then, ten minutes after she got off the phone, Lucy was fired by Columbia. She was out of a job.

Wait! WHAT?

But it was okay. Another studio—RKO—hired her and Lucy got a seven-year contract with *them*.

Anything for a Laugh

Lucy could have been just another pretty girl in the background, but she wanted to be a *real* movie star. So she worked really hard. She would hang around movie sets in case anybody needed a walk-on.

And she would volunteer to do *anything*. If they needed somebody to get a pie thrown in her face, she would do it. If they needed somebody to fall into a lake and get attacked by a crocodile, she would do it.

Wait. She got attacked by a crocodile?

Well, it was a trained crocodile that had no teeth, but I still think she was brave to say yes.

"I said I'd love to do the scene with the crocodile. He didn't have teeth, but he could sure gum you to death."

Lucy would wear a fright wig, a goatee, or a fake nose. She didn't mind getting locked in a meat freezer. One time she got shot out of a steamship funnel.

Most actresses didn't want to do scenes that were dangerous or would make them look silly. But Lucy loved it. She was getting noticed.

So then she got rich and famous, right?

No. She was getting small parts, but a lot of the time she didn't have any lines to say and she didn't even get a credit at the end of the movie. But she didn't give up. She kept trying, and she kept getting better.

I counted. In 1934, Lucy was in eleven movies. *Eleven!* That's almost one movie every month.

She would become famous on TV later, but most people don't know that she was in more than seventy movies before she began her TV career. And her parts were getting bigger and better. People started calling her "Queen of the Bs."

What's a B?

B movies were movies made with very little money, predictable plots, and actors and actresses who weren't very famous.

It sounds like B stood for *bad* movies.

Not always! Some of them were good. And Lucy appeared in all kinds of movies—comedies, dramas, musicals. She even auditioned to play Scarlett O'Hara in *Gone with the Wind*. But she didn't get the part.

She was one of the only actresses who appeared in movies with the Three Stooges, the Marx Brothers, and Abbott and Costello. But she was still a nobody, earning less than a hundred dollars a week.

Of course, back in those days it only cost fifty cents to go to the movies.

True, but Lucy wasn't making progress. One time she saw a casting sheet that called for an actress who was "a Lucille Ball type." She went to the audition, but she wasn't hired. They said she wasn't right for the part!

Ouch! That had to hurt.

But in 1942, everything changed.

Redhead

The biggest studio in Hollywood at the time was Metro-Goldwyn-Mayer. They made *The Wizard of Oz*, *Gone with the Wind*, and lots of other famous movies. All the biggest movie stars worked for MGM. The company slogan was "More stars than there are in heaven." In 1942, they signed Lucy. She was thirty-one.

And finally, she became a big movie star, right?

No.

No?

No. Do you know what was the first thing MGM did after they hired Lucy?

Shave off her eyebrows?

Yes! They also straightened her teeth and sent her to a coach to teach her how to lower her high, squeaky voice. They also told her to gain ten pounds.

Gain?

Yeah. Lots of actors and actresses have to worry about putting on too much weight. But Lucy was skinny. Her problem was keeping her weight *up*. So while the other actresses would chew on celery stalks, Lucy would wolf down a fried potato sandwich. Her favorite meal was a hamburger smothered in onions.

She was given a complete makeover when she got to MGM. And the biggest thing they did to her was change the color of her hair.

We said back in Chapter 3 that she dyed her hair from brown to blonde when she became a model.

Right. But the hairstylist at MGM decided she should be a redhead.

How come?

Lucy had big blue eyes. They really showed up with red hair. And also, movies had started using Technicolor, a system that used three strips of film and red and green filters to make colors look really vivid and vibrant.

"I was born for Technicolor."

So they sent her to a colorist. On the first attempt, somehow the chemicals in the dye reacted weirdly and Lucy's hair came out green. But they fixed that, and the finished product was more orange than red. She kept it that way for the next forty years. For the rest of her life, she was the world's most famous redhead.

"I didn't mind getting messed up. That's how I got into physical comedy."

CHAPTER 5

Lucy and Desi

We should back up just a little, to 1939. That's when Lucy first met this guy—

Uh-oh. I know what *this* means. Here comes the yucky part.

It's not yucky! Lucy fell in love!

Ugh!

Oh, grow up, Turner! Lucy was making movies and getting more well-known. She started shooting this movie called *Too Many Girls*. A handsome young guy from Cuba named Desi Arnaz played one of her bodyguards. They started going out, and a year later they eloped.

Isn't that illegal?

Why would eloping be illegal?

Because you cantaloupe. Get it? Cantaloupe? Can't elope?

That's totally not funny.

Well, you can't blame a guy for trying.

Anyway, most people don't know that Lucy and Desi lied about their ages on the marriage certificate. It says they were both twenty-six. But Lucy was really twenty-nine and Desi was twenty-three.

Why did they lie?

In those days, people thought it was strange for a woman to marry a man younger than she was.

The old days were *weird*. Hey, why do we have to do a whole section in the book about Lucy's husband? I thought the book was supposed to be about Lucy.

Desi Arnaz wasn't *just* her husband. They were a team. Trust me on this.

Okay, let's get it over with.

His full name was Desiderio Alberto Arnaz y de Acha III.

But everybody called him Desi.

He didn't grow up poor, like Lucy did. Desi's father was the mayor of Santiago de Cuba. His uncle was the chief of police. His grandfather was a doctor who traveled with Teddy Roosevelt and the Rough Riders.

TR! We wrote about him in *Teddy Roosevelt Was a Moose?!*

True. The Arnaz family owned three homes. Growing up, Desi even had his own speedboat. But then something horrible happened.

A speedboat accident?

No. One morning in the summer of 1933, Desi heard shouts and gunfire in the distance. There was a revolution going on. Anyone involved with the government was targeted.

So what did they do?

Desi's father was in Havana at the time. His mother grabbed their pet Chihuahua and they got out of there. As they ran away, Desi saw his house lit on fire. His family disguised themselves as revolutionaries and went into

50

hiding. A few months later, they escaped to Florida. But they had lost everything they owned.

Wow. So both Lucy and Desi's families lost everything at some point.

Right. Desi was seventeen years old, and he didn't speak English yet. But he was really ambitious. While he was going to high school in Florida, he earned money by walking dogs, driving a taxi, and cleaning canary cages in a pet store. At one point, he drove a banana truck.

They have trucks shaped like a banana?

No, dope! He drove a truck that *carried* bananas.

Oh, I knew that.

Desi was also a talented singer and guitar player. In 1936, he got a job playing in a rumba band at a Miami hotel. People liked him, so he decided to start his own band. They weren't very good, until Desi decided to try the popular Cuban song "La Conga." The audience forms a line and they dance their way around the room.

I've heard of conga lines.

It became a dance craze all over America. Desi was just twenty-two. He became an overnight sensation. He had never even seen a Broadway show, but soon he was the star of one, and it ran for seven months. After that, he started to appear in movies.

And that's when he met Lucy.

Right. They fell in love. And one November day in 1940, Lucy was being interviewed for a magazine article about why she liked being single. Desi showed up and said it was going to be a hard article to write. Lucy asked him why, and he said, "Because I have everything arranged to marry you tomorrow morning." Isn't that romantic?

No.

Well, how about this: When they were about to get married the next day, Desi realized that he forgot to get a wedding ring. So his manager ran to the local Woolworth's store and bought a brass ring from the costume jewelry counter.

And I suppose they lived happily ever after?

Honestly, they didn't. They loved each other, but Desi was on the road with his band a lot and he was hardly ever home. He also liked to drink, gamble, party, and stay out all night. Lucy and

Desi fought a lot. There were nights when Desi would pack his clothes and go to a hotel. It got to be pretty expensive. So you know what he did?

Yeah. He built himself a little house in their backyard where he would sleep when they were fighting.

How did you know that?

I told you. I did my research! And Lucy was fine with it, because at least it was a way to keep Desi at home.

If only there had been a project the two of them could work on *together*. Hmmmm.

Hmmmmm . . .

My Favorite Husband

People in the movie business were starting to freak out in the late 1940s. Radio was really popular and television was starting up. Instead of paying money to go out to a movie, a lot of people were staying home to listen to the radio and watch TV.

Lucy appeared on a lot of radio shows to make extra money, and she loved it. When she made a movie, she couldn't see the audience react. But performing in front of a live audience on air, she could see and hear people responding. And *laughing*.

In 1948, she was the star of a radio comedy called *My Favorite Husband*. It ran for 124 episodes, and CBS wanted to turn it into a TV show. Lucy thought it would be the perfect opportunity for her and Desi to work on something together. So she said she would do the TV show, but only if Desi—her real husband—could play her TV husband.

And the rest is history?

No, it's not. CBS didn't want Desi.

Why not?

Desi wasn't like anyone else on TV at that time. He didn't speak perfect English. He had a Cuban accent. CBS was afraid that people wouldn't accept Lucy and Desi as a married couple.

But they *were* a married couple!

What can I say? The good old days were messed up.

So what did Lucy and Desi do?

They put together an act and took it on the road to prove that people would like them as a couple. Desi played a bandleader who sang and played bongos. Lucy played his nutty wife who wants a job playing cello with the band.

Oh yeah! I saw that on YouTube. She had a trick cello with flowers and a toilet plunger hidden inside it. She used the strings of the cello to shoot the bow at Desi. It was hilarious.

At one point in the act, Lucy imitated a seal. She flopped around on her stomach and played a xylophone with her nose.

They did the act in theaters around the country, and people loved it. So CBS finally agreed to put Lucy and Desi together as husband and wife in their own TV show. And of course they called it . . .

"I believe that we're as happy in life as we make up our minds to be."

CHAPTER 6

I Love Lucy

Lucy and Desi combined their names and started their own company—Desilu Productions. They also named their house, their boat, and their station wagon "Desilu."

Desi was a good cook, and he even named his special goulash "Desilu."

But before they could start working on their TV show, something else was on their minds. On July 17, 1951, Lucy had a baby girl! They had decided in advance to name the baby "Susan" if it was a girl. So when Lucy woke up from aesthesia and was told she had a girl, she asked to see Susan. But while Lucy was asleep, Desi signed the birth certificate with the name "Lucie."

Why did he do that?

I guess he just had to have more than one Lucy in the family!

Anyway, just six weeks after Lucie Arnaz was born, the rehearsals for *I Love Lucy* began.

We should mention that it was like a different world in 1951. Hardly anybody had a TV back then. And *nobody* had a remote control. It hadn't been invented yet.

So how did they change the channel or adjust the volume?

They had to get up off the couch and turn a dial on the TV.

What? That's crazy!

Yeah, there was a lot less channel-flipping. There were also a lot less channels.

How many channels did they have?

Four.

Are you kidding me? How did they survive?

It must have been tough. Anyway, on the show, Lucy played Lucy Ricardo, a housewife who wants to get into show business. Desi played Ricky Ricardo, a bandleader a lot like himself. Their neighbors and landlords were Fred and

Ethel Mertz, who were played by the actors William Frawley and Vivian Vance.

I heard that in real life, Vivian Vance and William Frawley didn't like each other. He was twenty-two years older, and she said, "How can anyone believe I'm married to that old coot?" But they made a great pair on TV.

Lucy loved performing in front of a live audience on radio, so *I Love Lucy* was filmed in a studio with three hundred people. And I bet you don't know who was in the studio audience for every episode.

You're not so great yourself!

Humf!

Sure I do. It was Lucy's mother, DeDe! Sometimes you can even hear her laughing in the background.

I can't believe you knew that!

I know lots of stuff. Did you know that a few minutes before the first episode was shot, the Los Angeles health inspector came in and threatened to shut the studio down?

Why?

Because the ladies' bathroom was too far away from the studio audience.

So what did they do?

Lucy saved the day. She said the women in the studio audience could use the bathroom in her dressing room.

The first episode they filmed was titled "Lucy Thinks Ricky Is Trying to Murder Her." *I Love Lucy* went on the air on Monday night, October 15, 1951, at nine o'clock.

Queen of the John

Well, it was a *big* success, right away. Within a

month, fourteen million people were watching *I Love Lucy*. A month after that, it was sixteen million.

And this is a time when there were only about fifteen million television sets in the whole country!

Wait. How is it possible that sixteen million people were watching fifteen million TVs?

Because more than one person was watching each set. Not many people had TVs yet, so friends and families would gather around the TV to watch together. And most of them were watching *I Love Lucy*. Within six months, it was the number-one show in America. At some point, the weekly audience grew to thirty-one million people—nearly a fifth of the United States population.

Monday night at nine became "Lucy Time." Taxis disappeared from the streets of New York City because everybody was

watching *I Love Lucy*. The Marshall Field's department store in Chicago closed on Monday nights because nobody was shopping at that time. The number of telephone calls dropped during the half hour when *I Love Lucy* was on. Lucy was also called "Queen of the John."

Why?

Because water use dropped while *I Love Lucy* was on. People would wait until the show was over to go to the bathroom.

Classic Episodes

Lucy's character on *I Love Lucy* was sort of like everybody's next-door neighbor, but funnier. Here are a few of the most famous episodes of the show. We watched them all on YouTube . . .

"LUCY DOES A TV COMMERCIAL"
Season 1, Episode 30

Ricky is hosting a TV show, and Lucy tricks him into letting her do a commercial for a health tonic called "Vitameatavegamin." She doesn't realize the stuff contains twenty-three percent alcohol, and after a number of practice runs sipping it she's totally drunk, slurring her words and staggering around the studio.

"LUCY'S ITALIAN MOVIE"
Season 5, Episode 23

Lucy is in Rome, and she meets a director who needs a typical American tourist to play a part in a movie about the wine industry. She has to climb into a giant vat filled with grapes and stomp on them with her bare feet. Afterward, Lucy said, "It was like stepping on eyeballs." A local woman is stomping around in the vat too, and the two of them end up slipping, sliding, and wrestling in the grape juice.

Actually, Lucy almost drowned shooting that scene. The actress playing the local woman didn't speak English, and she held Lucy's head under the smashed grapes too long. Later, Lucy said, "I had grapes up my nose, up my ears. I thought it was my last moment on earth."

Still, it's hilarious.

"LUCY DOES THE TANGO"
Season 6, Episode 20

Lucy and Ricky decide to make money by raising chickens in their backyard. But the chickens don't lay any eggs, and Lucy doesn't want Ricky to find out. So she buys dozens of eggs at a store and hides them in her shirt when she goes out to the chicken coop. Then Desi shows up and says he wants to practice a tango for his nightclub act. They do the dance and all the eggs crack inside her shirt.

It was hysterical, of course, and the studio audience kept laughing for sixty-five seconds. It was one of the longest laughs the show ever got. It went on so long, they had to cut it in half when the episode was edited.

"JOB SWITCHING"
Season 2, Episode 1

This is probably the most familiar scene in *I Love Lucy*. Lucy and Ethel get jobs working in a candy factory. They have to wrap pieces of chocolate as they slide along a conveyor belt. The belt moves faster and faster until Lucy and Ethel can't keep up and they have to stuff the chocolates in their mouths, in their hats, and down their shirts.

I dare anybody to watch that one without laughing.

But there's one episode of *I Love Lucy* that was the most famous of all . . .

"Luck? I don't know anything about luck. Luck to me is something else: hard work—and realizing what is an opportunity and what isn't."

CHAPTER 7

Lucy Goes to the Hospital

Near the end of the first season of *I Love Lucy*, the real-life Lucille Ball found out that she was going to have another baby. At first, Lucy and Desi thought that meant the TV show was over. But their producer, Jess Oppenheimer, had another idea: "Why don't we continue the show and have a baby on TV?"

That was a revolutionary idea in the 1950s. You didn't see pregnant women on TV. Actors couldn't even say the word *pregnant* on TV. They had to say a woman was *expecting* or *with child*.

What's wrong with the word *pregnant*?

They thought it was inappropriate, for some reason.

Man, the good old days were *really* messed up!

Hey, there are words kids say all the time that would be considered inappropriate if they were in this book. Maybe someday it will all seem silly. Anyway, CBS didn't like the idea of Lucy being pregnant. But *I Love Lucy* was the most popular show in the country, and CBS finally agreed to make Lucy's pregnancy part of the show.

So Season 2 went along and Lucy's belly got bigger and bigger until she had the baby in Episode 16—"Lucy Goes to the Hospital." And it just so happened that the *real* Lucy gave birth on January 19, 1953, just twelve hours before TV

Lucy delivered their son, "Little Ricky."

The real baby—Desiderio Alberto Arnaz IV—was called Desi Jr. Little Ricky was played by twin child actors.

Lucy giving birth was probably the biggest thing to happen in the history of television. Ninety percent of the people who owned a TV watched the episode—forty-four million people!

Yeah, and the next day only twenty-nine million people watched President Eisenhower's inauguration.

Companies sold Little Ricky dolls, Lucy nursery tables, games, and jewelry. An *I Love Lucy* comic strip ran in 132 newspapers. You could even buy an *I Love Lucy* potty seat.

Lucy got thirty thousand letters and telegrams congratulating her.

What's a telegram?

It was like a letter that was delivered electronically.

You mean like a text or an email?

Sort of, but it was printed on paper.

So it was a letter.

Not exactly. The point is, it was Lucy*mania*! Desi Jr. and Lucy were on the cover of the first issue of *TV Guide*.

Actually, Lucy appeared on the cover of *TV Guide* thirty-nine times, more than anybody else.

Hey, I just noticed something. Lucy and Desi named their two kids Lucie and Desi!

"I'd rather regret things I've done than regret the things I haven't done."

CHAPTER 8

The Four-Headed Monster

I Love Lucy wasn't just the most popular TV show in the country. Lucy and Desi also made a bunch of decisions that changed the way television was made.

Oh yeah. Before *I Love Lucy*, most TV shows were made in New York City and they were shot live. But people on the West Coast are three hours behind New York, so they didn't see anything live. They watched kinescopes of the show a day or more later.

Kinescopes? What's a kinescope?

It was like pointing a camera at a TV screen and recording it. Kinescopes were cheap to make and the picture was fuzzy. CBS thought they would make *I Love Lucy* like all the other TV shows at the time.

But Lucy and Desi were living in California, and they wanted to keep their family there. So Desi came up with another idea: What if they shot *I Love Lucy* on *film*, the same way movies were made? The image quality would be much sharper than kinescopes, and they could send the prints to TV stations all over the country to broadcast them. So that's what they did.

Here's another smart decision they made. Back in those days, TV shows were shot using one camera. But on *I Love Lucy* they used *three* cameras, all filming at the same time. One camera shot close-ups, one was for medium shots, and one was for longer shots that included the whole set. It was a lot faster than shooting the same scene over and over again to get all the shots that were needed.

They also saved tons of time by using the "Four-Headed Monster." It was a machine that was able to hold the film from all three of those cameras so they could be easily edited.

If there were three cameras, why was it called the Four-Headed Monster?

The fourth head was just for the *sound*.

Oh. Another smart decision they made was to build a big stage with four different locations right next to one another. One location was Lucy and Desi's living room. The second one was their bedroom. The third one was Desi's nightclub. And the fourth one could be used for any other location they needed for the episode.

So the studio audience could sit in one place and watch the actors move across the stage to film all the scenes.

Exactly!

But here's the *biggest* decision Lucy and Desi made—they took a thousand-dollar pay cut to shoot *I Love Lucy* on film on the condition that Desilu would own each episode after it aired.

Why was that such a big deal?

Because episodes of *I Love Lucy* would be shown a *zillion* times! Lucy and Desi invented the rerun!

You mean before that it never occurred to

anybody that people might want to watch a TV show more than once?

Yes! And they've been running those *I Love Lucy* episodes for the last seventy years! They've been dubbed into more than twenty languages and shown in seventy-seven countries.

Wow! Those reruns must have made Lucy and Desi a ton of money.

Duh! And they used that money to make Desilu bigger. They developed other hit TV shows like *The Real McCoys*, *The Untouchables*, and *The Dick Van Dyke Show*. Desilu made hundreds of commercials too. It became the biggest TV studio in the world, with twenty-six sound stages and a thousand employees. Lucy and Desi became TV's first millionaires.

All those decisions were revolutionary when they were making *I Love Lucy*. Now almost all comedies are made that way. A lot of the credit goes to Lucy and Desi.

More fun facts we found about
I Love Lucy . . .

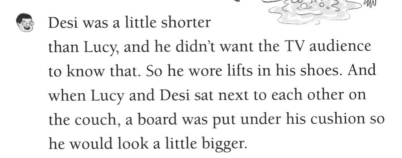

The first scripts for *I Love Lucy* abbreviated the name of the show to "ILL." Lucy took a look at the script and said, "I don't want a show that's ill." After that, the scripts just said "LUCY" on them.

The first week *I Love Lucy* was filmed, Lucy and Vivian Vance cleaned the bathrooms in the studio.

Yuck!

Show biz is gross!

Desi was a little shorter than Lucy, and he didn't want the TV audience to know that. So he wore lifts in his shoes. And when Lucy and Desi sat next to each other on the couch, a board was put under his cushion so he would look a little bigger.

The first episode of *I Love Lucy* was filmed on Desi's thirty-fourth birthday—March 2, 1951. But the film somehow disappeared and was missing for nearly forty years. One of Desi's friends, Pepito Perez, finally found a copy at his house, and it was aired in a special CBS tribute in 1990.

The first season of *I Love Lucy* was thirty-five episodes. These days, most TV shows are just ten or fifteen episodes.

During breaks from filming *I Love Lucy*, Lucy and Desi also acted in two movies together, *The Long, Long Trailer* and *Forever Darling*. In the first one, they played newlyweds driving cross-country in an RV.

The *I Love Lucy* Christmas episode was one of the first holiday specials in television history.

In one episode, Lucy promises Little Ricky she'll get Superman to come to his birthday party. George Reeves, who played Superman on TV, was a guest on that show. But Lucy didn't want Desi Jr. to know that Superman

WOW!

wasn't real. So she insisted that George Reeves's name didn't appear in the credits.

 Jay Sandrich was a twenty-one-year-old assistant director on *I Love Lucy*. He went on to direct lots of other classic comedies, such as *Make Room for Daddy*, *Get Smart*, *The Mary Tyler Moore Show*, *The Bob Newhart Show*, *The Odd Couple*, *The Cosby Show*, *The Golden Girls*, and *Two and a Half Men*.

"Love yourself first and everything else falls into line. You really have to love yourself to get anything done in this world."

CHAPTER 9

After *I Love Lucy*

In the 1950s, TV shows didn't run for ten or more seasons. *I Love Lucy* ended in 1957. It never ranked below third place during its six-year run.

Well, it didn't *completely* end. After it was over, Lucy and Desi did thirteen episodes of a show called *The Lucy-Desi Comedy Hour*. Their last show was on March 2, 1960. It was Desi's forty-third birthday. And do you know what Lucy and Desi did the next day?

They retired?

No. They got divorced.

Wait. WHAT? I thought they were the perfect couple! I thought they were made for each other! I thought they loved each other.

They did. But like we said earlier, they fought a lot. Lucy wanted a husband who would stay home with her and be a family man. Desi liked to gamble, drink, and chase other women. So they decided to split up.

Lucy received eight thousand letters begging her to patch things up with Desi, but she had made up her mind.

Two years later, Lucy bought out Desi's shares of Desilu Productions. He retired, and the board of directors asked Lucy to be president. So she became the first woman to run a major TV studio. Eventually she sold Desilu to Gulf + Western for seventeen million dollars. It was renamed Paramount Television.

That's a lot of coin! Hey, Turner, have you ever heard of *Star Trek* or *Mission Impossible*?

Of course. I love those movies.

Well, you can thank Lucy.

What? Why?

Back in the 1960s, the other bigwigs at Desilu had the chance to make the *Star Trek* and *Mission Impossible* TV shows. They turned both of them down.

How come?

Mainly because they would cost a lot of money to film. But Lucy was the president of the company. She overruled them, and gave the go-ahead to shoot both series. They became huge, and were turned into all those movies. But if it wasn't for Lucy, there would be no *Star Trek* or *Mission Impossible* today.

Lucy didn't really like being a TV executive. She

liked performing comedy in front of a live audience. After she and Desi split up, she did six seasons of another sitcom called *The Lucy Show*.

And after *that* was over, she did six seasons of *another* sitcom called *Here's Lucy*. She even had her kids on that one with her. Lucie was seventeen and Desi Jr. was fifteen.

And after *that* was over, she did *another* sitcom called *Life with Lucy*. But none of those shows had the magic of the original *I Love Lucy*.

Strange Stuff about Lucy

Let me start this part by saying that *all* of us act a little strange sometimes. Like, if you look at our lives really closely, we have all done some strange stuff.

So I guess you're going to tell us some strange stuff about Lucy.

Yeah. Like she was good friends with the actress

84

Carole Lombard. After Lombard died in a plane crash in 1942, Lucy became afraid of flying.

What's so strange about that? Lots of people don't like to fly.

Yeah, but when Lucy was on a plane, she was known to get out of her seat and clean the floors and toilets.

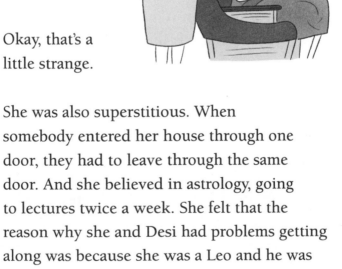

I'll take some peanuts, a mop, and broom if you have it.

Okay, that's a little strange.

She was also superstitious. When somebody entered her house through one door, they had to leave through the same door. And she believed in astrology, going to lectures twice a week. She felt that the reason why she and Desi had problems getting along was because she was a Leo and he was a Pisces.

That's pretty strange. But millions of people believe in astrology.

How about this one? Desi's last name was Arnaz, and Lucy was convinced that the letters *A* and *R* were good luck. That's why she chose the last names "RicARdo" and "CARmichael" for the characters she played on TV.

Hmmmm.

Okay, this is the strangest one of all. Remember back in the beginning of the book when I told you that Lucy could pick up radio signals through her teeth?

Yeah. I said you were crazy.

Well, it was *true*! One day she went to the dentist and he filled some cavities for her. Afterward, Lucy started hearing strange sounds and music. She didn't know where they were coming from. Then she realized the sound was coming from her own mouth! Her fillings were picking up mysterious radio waves!

86

I suppose it was aliens who wanted to audition for *I Love Lucy*.

Very funny. She contacted the FBI, and they traced the sounds to an underground radio station run by a Japanese gardener!

Okay, I admit it. *That's* strange.

Oops!

Hey Paige! Let's play a game.

I love games!

Good. Performing physical comedy can be dangerous, and Lucy was pretty accident-prone. I'm going to give you a list of bad things that may or may not have happened to her. You have to guess which ones I made up, and which ones actually happened to Lucy in real life.

That sounds like fun. Go ahead.

Okay, here's my list . . .

1. She fell stepping into a rowboat, landed on her face, was knocked unconscious, and had a concussion.
2. She was talking to somebody on a ski slope when another skier lost control and crashed into her. Her leg was broken in four places.
3. She was bruised all over doing a chase scene in which tons of coffee beans landed on her.
4. A horse stomped on her foot and hurt her toes so badly that she had to wear open-toed shoes from then on.
5. She got temporary paralysis in her eyeball after talcum powder was blown into her face by a wind machine.
6. She mysteriously started stuttering for no reason.

uh oh!

7. She was asked to do a pratfall on ice skates, but she fell over backward, landed on her back, was carried off on a stretcher, and spent the next ten days in the hospital.

Okay, which of those are real and which ones are fake?

Hmmmm. This is a tough one. I'd say numbers 1, 2, and 7 are real, and 3, 4, 5, and 6 are fake.

You're wrong. They *all* happened to Lucy!

Wait! WHAT? For real?

Hey, everything in this book is true. That's why they call it a biography! I can't believe she survived all that stuff.

The secret to staying young is to live honestly, eat slowly, and lie about your age.

CHAPTER 10

Oh Yeah? (Stuff About Lucille Ball That Didn't Fit Anywhere Else)

Okay, what do you have left in your notes, Turner?

Let me see. Oh, I know something you don't know, Paige. The Arnaz family was very musical. Desi was a professional bandleader and singer before *I Love Lucy*. And his band played the *I Love Lucy* theme song. On the TV show nobody is singing. But the lyrics were . . .

I love Lucy and she loves me,
We're as happy as two can be.
Sometimes we quarrel but then
How we love making up again.

That reminds me, Lucy didn't have a great voice, but she had a hit song of her own. She popularized the song "Hey, Look Me Over" from her Broadway show *Wildcat*.

When he was just eleven, Desi Jr. started a rock-and-roll group called Dino, Desi & Billy. Dino was the son of the famous entertainer Dean Martin. The group even went on tour and had a hit song, "I'm a Fool." And his sister Lucie Arnaz was an actress and a singer who appeared in many musicals, like *They're Playing Our Song* and *My One and Only*.

Even William Frawley, who played Fred Mertz on *I Love Lucy*, was a singer. You can listen to his album on Spotify—*Bill Frawley Sings the Old Ones*.

And speaking of William Frawley, he was a big New York Yankees fan. He had it written into his contract that he didn't have to go to work if the Yankees were playing in the World Series— which they were in 1951, 1952, 1953, 1955, and 1956.

And speaking of Desi Jr., like his dad, he was a bit of a playboy. When he was young he dated the stars Liza Minnelli and Patty Duke.

When she wasn't working, Lucy loved to play charades, Scrabble, Monopoly, poker, and especially backgammon. She also enjoyed crocheting, painting, and gardening.

Lucy loved animals. She had a poodle named Tinker Bell and fox terriers named Toy and Whoopee.

During World War II, Lucy and Desi thought they could get around food shortages by raising their own animals for meat. But they became attached to the animals and couldn't bring themselves to slaughter them. When their cow got sick, Desi wrapped it in blankets and warmed it with hot-water bottles. The cow was so grateful that it smashed through their bedroom window to give Desi a kiss.

They also had multiple cats, a four-hundred-pound pig, three roosters, and three hundred baby chicks.

Lucy's career almost ended after the first season of *I Love Lucy*. It was the height of the Cold War and lots of Hollywood celebrities were "blacklisted" because they were suspected of being disloyal to America. In fact, Lucy registered as a Communist when she twenty-five. But she explained that she never voted Communist and only registered as a Communist because her grandfather told her to. The FBI cleared her and the scandal didn't hurt Lucy's career.

It probably helped that she was the most famous and beloved woman in America at the time.

I bet you don't know the name of the one actor who appeared in every one of Lucy's TV shows.

Uh, Lucille Ball?

Yes, but who else?

No clue.

It was Gale Gordon. He appeared in *I Love Lucy*, *The Lucy Show*, *Here's Lucy*, and *Life with Lucy*. He was even on her radio show *My Favorite Husband*.

Oh yeah? I bet *you* didn't know that Desi was

famous for his spaghetti sauce. One day at a dinner party, he came out of the kitchen with a big pot of it and announced that dinner was ready. The bottom of the pot suddenly collapsed and all the sauce landed on the rug. For a moment, the guests just stared. Then they grabbed their plates and served themselves off the floor. That's how good Desi's sauce was.

Oh yeah? I bet you didn't know that Lucy's grandmother Flora Belle was one of *five* sets of twins. Can you imagine what *that* house was like?

Animated Lucy appeared on *The Simpsons* three times. In one episode, Lisa gets visited by Lucy's ghost. In another episode, Moe sells clams that look like Lucy. Finally, one of the characters visits Lucy's grave in a parody called *I Lost Lucy*.

Dressing up like Lucy is a thing. In the movie *Rat Race*, a bus driver is trapped on his bus filled with Lucy look-alikes. And in 2011, 915 Lucy impersonators came to her hometown of Jamestown, New York, to celebrate Lucy's one hundredth birthday.

Jamestown *loves* Lucy. The Lucille Ball Desi Arnaz Museum is there. In the gift shop, you can buy Lucy coasters, spoons, plates, shirts, dresses, aprons, coffee mugs, key chains, pillows, refrigerator magnets, clocks, salt and pepper shakers, cookbooks, and shower curtains.

You don't have to go to Jamestown to buy Lucy stuff. There's an online Lucy Store that sells twenty-five hundred Lucy items. They even have a "Super Lucy" clothing line—with a

picture of Lucy dressed up like
Superman flying with Desi in
her arms.

Just outside Jamestown is a
park that has a statue of Lucy.
It was put there in 2009, but it
was so strange-looking that people nicknamed it
"Scary Lucy." In 2016, a prettier statue was
made to replace the first one. But Scary Lucy
had become such a tourist attraction that it was
decided to keep *both* statues in the park. They
are seventy-five yards away from each other.

There are only a few more pages in the book.
You know what that means.

What?

It means Lucy's going to die.

How do you know?

It's a biography! The person *always* dies at the end.

What if it's a living person?

I think they wait until people die before doing a biography of them.

Well, Lucy didn't die just yet. After *I Love Lucy* went off the air, she kept working. She starred in a Broadway musical, and she acted in some movies, such as *Mame* and *Stone Pillow*, where she played an old homeless woman.

She even taught a course in TV and film at California State University.

We should mention that she got married again too. She married a comedian named Gary Morton. In fact, they were married longer than she was married to Desi Arnaz.

But Lucy and Desi stayed friends for the rest of their lives. Desi was a smoker, and he got lung cancer in 1986. Near the end, Lucy visited him and they watched old videos of *I Love Lucy* together. He was just sixty-nine when he died.

As she got older, Lucy was showered with awards and honors. She was inducted into the National Women's Hall of Fame, and she was the first female inductee to the Television Hall of Fame. The street where she was born was renamed Lucy Street.

Here it comes.

Yeah, I guess I can't stall any longer. Like Desi, Lucy was a longtime smoker. She had angina, high blood pressure, a stroke, and heart surgery. She was seventy-seven when she died on April 26, 1989. When she was in the hospital, she received five thousand get-well cards a day.

There were memorial services in New York, Los Angeles, and Chicago. All three of them started at nine o'clock on a Monday night—the same time *I Love Lucy* used to come on the air. She's buried in Lake View Cemetery in her hometown, Jamestown, New York.

And do you know what it says on the garbage cans in that cemetery?

No. What?

I Love Lucy.

TO FIND OUT MORE . . .

Did we get you interested in the life of Lucille Ball? Yay! If you want to find out more, there are also lots of videos about Lucille Ball on YouTube. And you can stream old episodes of *I Love Lucy*, which are just as funny today as they were in the 1950s.

ACKNOWLEDGMENTS

Thanks to Simon Boughton, Kristin Allard, Liza Voges, Allison Steinfeld, and Nina Wallace. The facts in this book came from various books, websites, and the National Comedy Center (which happens to be in Jamestown, New York). Especially helpful were *Ball of Fire* by Stefan Kanfer, *Lucille: The Life of Lucille Ball* by Kathleen Brady, and Lucille Ball's autobiography, *Love, Lucy*.

ABOUT THE AUTHOR

Dan Gutman has written many books for young readers, such as the My Weird School series, The Genius Files series, the Flashback Four series, *Houdini and Me*, *The Kid Who Ran For President*, *The Homework Machine*, *The Million Dollar Shot*, and his baseball card adventure books. Dan and his wife, Nina, live in New York City. You can find out more about Dan and his books by visiting his website (www.dangutman.com) or following him on Facebook, Twitter, and Instagram.

TITLES IN THE

Wait! *WHAT?*

SERIES